# THE MEDITERRANEAN WAY
# TO LOSE
# WEIGHT

— *The Biochemical Basis of* —

**PRINCE N. AGBEDANU, PHD**

Text Copyright © 2022 by Prince N. Agbedanu

All rights reserved. No part of this guide may be reproduced in any form without permission in writing from the publisher except in the case of brief quotations embodied in critical articles or reviews.

**Legal & Disclaimer**

The information in this book and its contents is not designed to replace or take the place of any form of medical or professional advice. It is not meant to replace the need for independent medical, financial, legal or other professional advice or services as may be required. The content and information in this book have been provided for educational purposes only.

The content and information contained in this book have been compiled from sources deemed reliable, and it is accurate to the best of the author's knowledge, information and belief. However, the author cannot guarantee its accuracy and validity and cannot be held liable for errors and omissions. Furthermore, changes are periodically made to this book as and when needed. Where appropriate or necessary, you must consult a professional (including but not limited to your doctor, attorney, financial advisor or other professional advisors) before using any of the suggested remedies, techniques, or information in this book.

Upon using the contents and information in this book, you agree to hold harmless the Author from and against any damages, costs, and expenses, including any legal fees resulting from applying any of the information provided. This disclaimer applies to any loss, damages or injury caused by the use and application, whether directly or indirectly, of any advice or information presented, whether for breach of contract, tort, negligence, personal injury, criminal intent, or under any other cause of action.

You agree to accept all risks of using the information presented in this book.

You agree that by continuing to read this book, where appropriate or necessary, you shall consult a professional (including but not limited to your doctor, attorney, financial advisor or such other advisor as needed) before using any of the suggested remedies, techniques, or information in this book.

Book Design: Nonon Tech & Design

ISBN: 978-1-959642-08-4

# TABLE OF CONTENTS

INTRODUCTION ............................................................ 1

CHAPTER ONE: The Mediterranean Culture and its Influence on the Diet ........................................................ 11

CHAPTER TWO: Health Benefits of the Mediterranean Diet .............................................................................. 37

CHAPTER THREE: Meal Plans and Shopping List of Mediterranean Diet ........................................................ 43

CHAPTER FOUR: The Mediterranean Diet Recipes ..... 59

CHAPTER FIVE: The Mediterranean Diet Promotes Consistency as a Lifestyle ................................................ 81

CONCLUSION ............................................................ 85

REFERENCES .............................................................. 89

# INTRODUCTION

Many people are faced with the challenges of losing weight, eating healthily, and making healthy lifestyle choices. However, the biochemical basis for weight loss and living healthily does not immediately become apparent to many. By understanding these principles, we can be more motivated in our food choices. Research has shown that obesity and unhealthy weight gain are serious health problems for people in the United States of America and the world at large [1]. Thus, various means to promote proper nutrition and a good diet plan could be adopted for weight loss and healthy living. The Mediterranean diet is the focal point of this book since it is one of the healthiest nutritional plans to adopt for weight loss, proper nutrition, and healthy living.

This definitive guide aims to extensively discuss the history and cultural influence of the Mediterranean diet, the principles guiding the nutritional plan, its role in weight loss and other health benefits, the key ingredients of the diet, and the various meal plan, recipes, etc. But before these, it addresses the general principle of losing excess fat.

## WHAT IS THE MEDITERRANEAN DIET?

The Mediterranean Diet is a nutritional plan that is developed from the traditional meals of people around the Mediterranean Sea, such as in Greece, Italy, Spain, and Israel [2]. This diet is plant-based and involves a daily intake of fruits, vegetables, olive oil, nuts, whole grains, beans, other legumes, herbs, and spices [3]. However, other foods in this diet, such as animal proteins, are eaten in smaller amounts, with fish and seafood being the preferred animal proteins [4].

With frequent indecisions about what to eat or not to eat to stay healthy and lose weight, this diet plan is sustainable and offers flexibility in food choices. Historically, the regions bordering the Mediterranean Sea have differed in cultural practices and host 23 countries, including Greece,

Italy, Spain, Turkey, France, Israel, Lebanon, and the North African countries. Though there are variations in which foods are traditional and peculiar to a specific country, there is a considerable difference that creates room to choose from a range of healthy and nutritious meals to lose weight and improve general health.

## WHY YOU SHOULD FOLLOW THE MEDITERRANEAN DIET FOR WEIGHT LOSS:

**It is easy to follow:** Most diets involve tracking calories, completely removing specific foods or food groups, and counting macronutrients, but the Mediterranean Diet is more of a flexible diet that does not outline what not to eat. This diet plan is more sustainable because its principles emphasize what to eat more [5]. The biochemical basis of this diet involves eating more fruits, vegetables, nuts, seeds, whole grains, beans, and healthy oils to lose weight and maintain health [5].

**It is rated as the overall best diet in the world:** Yearly, the U.S. News & World Report ranks some of the best diets in the world, and the Mediterranean Diet is consecutively ranked as the best overall diet. For insight, Chef V was one of the experts featured in the 2022 review process of the world's best diets. Do you know what it means to show up atop? Explicitly, the difference between most fad diets and the Mediterranean Diet is that it is more sustainable and flexible [6]. You can and should follow this diet for more than just a few weeks or months to experience weight loss. In recent times, research has shown that many people who follow weight loss diets to shed some pounds usually regain that weight even more once they discontinue the diet. The good news remains that this nutrition emphasizes meal plans and accepts all healthy food groups, which makes it easy to follow and sustain over time.

**It is cost-effective and budget-friendly:** Plant-based foods are usually more affordable than animal products. Thus, a Mediterranean eating pattern may be more cost effective for your budget and economic situation. Although, certain Mediterranean foods, such as shelled pistachios, fresh artichokes, and artisan olive oils, may be expensive to sustain.

However, that should not discourage you from healthy eating and enjoying the benefits of a Mediterranean diet. To overcome this problem, when you draft your Mediterranean shopping list, ensure to include ingredients such as frozen vegetables, canned fish, dried beans, fruits, and whole grains that are relatively affordable and Mediterranean Diet-friendly.

**It is beneficial for the planet:** Plant-based diets more friendly for the environment because they have minimal contribution to global warming [7].

**It can be incorporated into any dish:** This diet can be included in any cuisine, and you don't have to live in Greece, Turkey, Italy, or Spain to reap the benefits of this healthy and nutritious way of eating. The only difference may be that Mediterranean people can easily get freshly pressed olive oil and seafood. Still, the various health-conscious supply chains and modern grocery stores ensure an easy and optimal supply of these foods without traveling miles to the Mediterranean. The keynote of this diet and its biochemical significance is that it focuses on food groups instead of specific foods. Therefore, you don't even have to be a fan of Spanish cuisine, Greek menus, or Italian dishes to follow and sustain this healthy way of eating.

## HOW DO WE LOSE EXCESS FATS?

Fats are categorized into three main groups: Fats, phospholipids, and some steroids[8]. The phospholipids make up the membranes (coverings) of our body cells; the steroids constitute several hormones, and the fats are stored as energy in the form of triglycerides[9]. When we consume both carbohydrates and fats, the body prefers to use carbohydrates and store the fats as reserved energy. Apart from serving as reserved energy, it also generates heat and protects or cushions the body's organs [9]. When carbohydrate levels become low, the body uses fat stores. Most diets rely on this principle: starve the body of carbohydrates and force the body to use the fat stores for energy production[10].

The fats are broken down by the enzyme called lipase (hormone-sensitive lipase). A small proportion of people

(1/1000,000) do not have lipases in their bodies due to a genetic disease. These individuals need external sources of lipase enzymes to enhance their metabolism. The free fatty acids released by lipases get into your muscles and are broken down in cycles called beta-oxidation to produce acetyl-coA (a 2-carbon molecule), which enters the citric acid cycle to yield ATP and other reducing equivalents. Consequently, fats are broken down into fatty acids, acetyl-coA, and carbon dioxide (in a biochemical process called decarboxylation), which exits the body when we exhale.

The hormone-sensitive lipase (HSL) needed to break down fats is known to become more active during exercise[11]. Consequently, the efficient breakdown of fats depends on activating the HSL during physical activity. Several positive changes in our organs are reported during physical activity. As we exercise, the heart pumps faster and more blood gets to all regions effectively. This blood carries nutrients to trillions of cells, allowing them to harness ATP (energy) from the nutrients. All cells need this energy to carry out their survival processes. This suggests that when blood circulation is not efficient (in the absence of exercise), nutrient delivery to some body regions may become less efficient, resulting in certain cells not receiving the nutrient they need to generate ATP [12, 13].

Consequently, these cells either start dying or attain a disease condition. Physical activity or exercise plays two key roles: activate hormone-sensitive lipase to break down fat (triglycerides) into free fatty acids and glycerol and facilitate the distribution of nutrients to all cells for them to make ATP for survival processes.

The diet that allows the storage of just enough fat or discourages the storage of fat has been the Mediterranean diet due to its core ingredients (discussed later in the chapters) and the culture of portion size [3]. It is essential to know that some people have a rare genetic condition called hyperphagia due to a mutation in a gene, which encodes the receptor for sensing the fed state[14]. A mutation in this receptor affects eating habits. Leptin is another hormone that regulates appetite. When the leptin receptor, LEPR, is bound by leptin, appetite is inhibited and cravings for food stops. It is called an appetite suppressant as the brain interprets leptin binding to the leptin receptor as satiety (that the stomach is full) and does not need more food [15]. When this receptor fails to respond to the presence of leptin, the individual is unable to feel satisfied but continues to eat; fat stores get filled with calories, and obesity is the consequence [16]. "Obesogenic environments": environments full of calorie-rich foods which tempt the individual to continue to eat are also causes of obesity.

When a diet fails to enforce portion size and lacks the core ingredients that discourage the storage of calories, the result is excess calories stored as fats. Under such circumstances, it becomes necessary to cut calories to reset eating habits hopefully. By the rule of thumb, eating according to portion sizes reduces an average of 500 calories daily. This cumulatively cuts 3500 Kilocalories from the diet per week, resulting in the loss of one pound per week. It follows that an average of 4 pounds can be lost in a month without having to starve oneself or deprive oneself of nutrients. Males require an average of 2500 kilocalories, while females require an average of 2000 kilocalories daily. Of the 2500 kilocalories for males, approximately 1700 to 1900 is required to maintain the individual's basal metabolic rate (heart rate and metabolism). That leaves 600-800 kilocalories for physical activity and the thermal effect of food (energy needed to digest food). That means 500 kilocalories can be safely cut when eaten by portion size. Cutting 500 kilocalories will not interfere with the required calorie for basal energy metabolism.

Similarly, on average, women need 2000 kilocalories per day, including 1200 to 1400, to maintain basal energy metabolism. That leaves 600-800 Kilocalories for physical activity and the thermal effect of food. Of these 600 to 800 kilocalories, 500 kilocalories can be safely cut by portion size without interfering with calories needed for basal energy metabolism. The Mediterranean diet accommodates the loss of these 500 kilocalories without the need to choose to lose them. It ensures portion size to promote the careful elimination of calories gradually without necessarily starving oneself [17]. To avoid counting calories, the Mediterranean way is the way to lose calories.

CHAPTER ONE:

# THE MEDITERRANEAN CULTURE AND ITS INFLUENCE ON THE DIET

In the 1960s, researchers found that people in the Mediterranean region experienced significantly lower mortality rates and chronic health conditions, including obesity, heart disease, stroke, and diabetes. There was a need to find out the potential factors that contributed to these lower rates of disease in that region, such as diet, social impacts, and physical activity. Years of studies showed that Mediterranean people ate various healthy, whole, minimally processed, and plant-based foods, which contributed to their healthy weight, lower rate of health complications, and long and healthy life [3, 9, 18, 19].

The Mediterranean diet represents the eating style of people in the olive-growing regions of Crete, Greece, and southern Italy in the late 1950s and early 1960s. According to the leading Mediterranean diet researcher Antonia Trichopoulou, MD, PhD, who is also the president of the Hellenic Health Foundation and director of the World Health Organization (WHO) Collaborating Center for Nutrition at the University of Athens (Greece) School of Medicine, the late 1950s and early 1960s is the era. At that time, the region surmounted the economic difficulties of post-World War II, and the people had sufficient healthy food to eat before the socioeconomic influences introduced more meat, processed foods, and vegetable oils into people's eating plans.

## THE OLDWAY MEDITERRANEAN DIET PYRAMID:

In 1993, Oldway designed the Mediterranean Diet Pyramid as an improved substitute to the USDA's archetype food pyramid, in affiliation with the Harvard School of Public

Health and the World Health Organization. Presently, the Mediterranean Diet is increasingly gaining popularity and patronage, with new research frequently discovering and updating its benefits [20]. At the base of the Mediterranean Diet pyramid, there is a strong emphasis on social connection and activity [21]. From the base upward, there are essential foods to get and enjoy daily, such as fruits, vegetables, whole grains, nuts, beans, herbs, spices, and healthy fats such as olive oil [22]. Fish and seafood are primarily consumed at least twice a week, and dairy foods, especially fermented dairy like yogurt and traditional cheese, are regularly consumed in moderate amounts [23]. Eggs and occasional poultry are allowed in the Mediterranean Diet, but red meat and sweets are seldomly eaten. Water and wine are the accepted beverages in the Mediterranean Diet for people who drink.

## HOW THE MEDITERRANEAN CULTURE INFLUENCED A DIET

Due to its popularity, you must have come across the Mediterranean diet in social gatherings, on the media, and in hospitals. Many doctors and healthcare providers may even recommend it for people with chronic conditions, including heart disease, diabetes mellites, and high blood pressure [24, 25, 26]. The biochemical implications of this diet often improve health and reduce the risk factors for obesity, heart disease, high cholesterol level, and dementia [3, 27].

There are diverse versions of the Mediterranean diet since the traditional foods of people around the Mediterranean Sea vary relatively across regions and cultures. In 1993, the Harvard School of Public Health, Oldways Preservation and Exchange Trust, and the European Office of the World Health Organization adopted the Mediterranean Diet Pyramid as a guide to help people determine the most common foods in this region [28]. Being more of a flexible eating plan than a strictly regulated diet plan, the pyramid outlined specific foods based on the traditional foods of Crete, Greece, and southern Italy in the mid-20$^{th}$ century. It was firmly believed that the underlying biochemical roles of the critical ingredients of this diet, mainly fruits and vegetables, fish, beans, nuts, seeds, whole grains, olive oil, small amounts of dairy, and red wine, are ideal for healthy cellular conditions, and contributed significantly to their weight loss, good health, and longevity [29]. The Mediterranean diet pyramid also specified daily exercise and the effective social benefits of eating meals together.

## KEY PRINCIPLES OF THE MEDITERRANEAN DIET:

In the dietary aspect, this isn't a strictly regulated diet. Still, certain foods are allowed, and others are either limited or entirely avoided. These recommendations are based on the Mediterranean Diet Pyramid [23]. Intending to lose weight, this diet aims to consume various fruits, vegetables, beans, nuts, whole grains, seeds, and healthy oils daily. Eat animal proteins, such as eggs, fish, poultry, and dairy, sparingly in a week. The acceptable beverages are wine (if you drink alcohol), coffee, water, and tea.

The core principles of this diet include cooking simple meals from fresh and minimally processed ingredients at home, which makes this the foundation of the traditional Mediterranean eating style [30]. The Mediterranean eating pattern is balanced and includes meat, occasional treats, and wine in moderate portions [24]. The diet is flexible and healthy, making it a sustainable approach to eating healthily. The diet contains relatively high-fat content that mainly comes from olive oil and tree nuts. In terms of usage, it is highly accepted and followed by most of the population for its health benefits, cost-effectiveness, and sustainability. Martínez-González states that the chemical role of the eating pattern comes from the long and successful culinary tradition of the Mediterranean diet.

The traditional Mediterranean diet emphasizes the intake of conventional foods, but if you're not local to the Mediterranean, then you could adjust your diet to the principles of the standard Mediterranean diet, according to Trichopoulou, another Dietician. Furthermore, they both agreed that in addition to its health-promoting effects, this diet is also palatable, as acknowledged by many people who adopted its variations [5].

## KEY INGREDIENTS OF THE MEDITERRANEAN DIET:

The Mediterranean diet is beyond just a variety of foods and nutrients. It is an integral part and reflection of Mediterranean history and culture. It also emphasizes home cooking using local or traditional ingredients, ensuring that not all foods linked with the region are used everywhere bordering the Mediterranean Sea. Although every Mediterranean country has its distinct foods and cuisines, the different foods offer similar nutrients, so the biochemical influence of its bioactive compounds is identical across cultures.

The Mediterranean diet offers a flavourful template for integrating healthy plant-based meals. Whole grains and legumes are widely available in many parts of the world, and so are garlic, capers, lemons, Feta, and plain yogurt. The herbs that offer various flavours and a phytonutrient effect to Mediterranean meals are also amazing additions to the diet plan, which makes it easy and inexpensive to convert them into a kitchen staple. Aim for the more deeply colored, more robust, sharp, or bitter greens, whether raw or cooked, rather than the paler ones. You can grow Italian dandelion and arugula seeds if you have a vegetable garden. Eventually, you'll be able to harvest them like the wild greens in Greece.

Olive trees, vineyards, and wheat have been found in the Mediterranean countries from inception. However, since the region is a geographical point of meeting for several different cultures, religions, and traditions, the typical and classic Mediterranean foods include those native to a certain area and those adopted years ago.

To save you the stress of having to travel to Greece, Spain, or Italy in search of key ingredients to enjoy their biochemical role-engendered benefits, below are some of the core foods and key ingredients in this toothsome, nutritious, and health-impacting diet.

**Olives:** Table olives, especially Kalamata olives, are excellent sources of antioxidant polyphenols [31]. The antioxidant polyphenols have excess electrons, which they donate to free radicals to stabilize them [32]. Consequently, they counter the effect of free radicals generated during various chemical reactions in the body [33]. Olives are globally used for cooking and flavouring. Add pitted olives in a food processor with olive oil, garlic, and your desired seasonings for a simple tapenade that produces a delicious sandwich spread, dip, or topping for poultry and fish. Freely toss pasta (cooked al dente) with chopped olives, garlic, olive oil, tomatoes, and fresh herbs of your desire. Include chopped olives in your desired tuna or chicken salad recipe.

**Olive Oil:** Italy, Greece, and Spain are the top three producers of olive oil. Olive oil is a key ingredient in the differing dietary plans encompassing the overall Mediterranean diet [2]. The biochemical profile, as shown by research, specifies that Extra-virgin olive oil is rich in carotenoids, tocopherols, and polyphenols, which are potent antioxidant and anti-inflammatory properties [33]. Olive oil is the primary source of dietary fat and is recommended in various diets involving vegetables and legumes. Olive oil is also used for baking and cooking. Contrary to common misconceptions, high-quality extra-virgin olive oil has a high smoke point due to its lower free fatty acid property. It also contains Vitamin E, an antioxidant that stabilizes free radicals generated during chemical reactions in the cells and maintains membrane integrity. A study on nutrition from Harvard states that Vitamin E can protect cells from free radical damage and reduce the production of free radicals in certain situations.

**Wheat:** This is the cornerstone grain of the Mediterranean [34], and contains adequate proteins, vitamins (notably B vitamins), dietary fibers, and phytochemicals. Wheat flour has approximately 13 times less sugar compared to yellow corn, according to the nutritional contents of wheat flour versus cooked yellow corn (100g each), using the 2020 USDA and NIH data. It also has high levels of niacin, folate thiamin, and riboflavin, although yellow corn has higher levels of Vitamin B6. By the same token, it surprisingly contains higher protein levels than corn. The role of B vitamins is primarily to help the body harness ATP from food. They contain coenzymes, molecules responsible for neutralizing acetic acid, converting them to acetyl-coA. acetyl-CoA is the central intermediate molecule produced during the digestion of all macronutrients. During Kreb's cycle, AcetylCOA combines with oxaloacetate to form citrate. It is also called the citric acid cycle. The rich source of vitamins in wheat allows the effective extraction of nutrients from food. A traditional grain called farro/emmer (Triticum dicoccum) is an ancient and classic wheat with regenerated popularity in Italy and the United States [35]. Bulgur is obtained from whole wheat berries that are steamed, dried, cracked, and used in tabbouleh, pilafs, and kibbe, a traditional Lebanese dish prepared with minced meat, bulgur, and spices. When choosing bulgur, select coarse for pilafs, medium for tabbouleh and other salads, and fine for kibbe. Bread equally uses unrefined wheat and barley flours. At the same time, Durum which has a creamy yellow colour that stems from the natural carotenoids is the milestone Mediterranean wheat used for couscous, bread, and Italian pasta. In the traditional eating pattern, wheat is ground with millstones to produce a fibre-rich whole wheat flour with a lower glycemic index than refined flour today. Wheat also was leavened with sourdough starter, and the fermentation lowered the glycemic index of the wheat flour and promoted digestibility.

**Lemons:** USDA sources for nutritional information show that lemons contain flavonoids that serve as antioxidants and decrease oxidative stress [36]. Acidic foods reduce glycemic response by delaying stomach emptying. The acidity and high flavonoid properties of lemon peels may have a biochemical role in blood glucose and help to control and prevent diabetes [37]. Lemons and oranges originated from the Far East, and the Arabians initially took them to the Mediterranean region. A typical Mediterranean practice is squeezing the lemons on salads, soups, fish, beans, or drinking water to reduce the meal's glycemic index. Lemon juice is another staple ingredient in hummus, and you can squeeze the juice over roasted broccoli or utilize it as the acid in a vinaigrette.

**Wild Greens:** USDA sources for nutritional information and NIH data show that wild greens contain carotenoids, vitamins C, vitamin E, and minerals, including iron, magnesium, and calcium, with antioxidant properties [38]. Savory pies, tortes, or tortas are prepared with greens, a staple cuisine in Greece, southern France, Italy, and other regions of the Mediterranean [39]. Dandelion greens, cardoon, rocket (arugula), fennel, purslane, and chicory, to mention a few, though there are over 150 types of wild greens on just the Greek island of Ikaria. The exact nutritional composition differs between species and cultivars. Still, wild, and dark leafy greens are loaded with carotenoids, vitamins C, vitamin E, and minerals like iron, magnesium, iron, and calcium [39]. They are rich in flavonoids, and eating a variety of greens is recommended. Greens also contain plant-based omega-3 fatty acids. In North America, edible wild greens are dandelion greens, purslane, and nutrient-dense cultivated greens like kale, mustard greens, beet greens, and collard greens. Add greens to frittatas, beans, scrambled eggs, and lentil soups. Sauté greens with garlic, top with a squeeze of lemon, and have some raw salads of dark leafy greens that are dressed with an olive oil vinaigrette, with or before eating.

**Capers:** Data collected by standard research engines such as Web of Science, SciFinder, PubMed, ScienceDirect, and Scopu showed that although caper is known for its sharp and robust flavor, it contains alkaloids, flavonoids, and steroids, all of which have antioxidant properties [40]. They are generally used as a flavourful and antioxidant-dense seasoning or garnish. Capers are a key ingredient in tapenade and are frequently added to salads. Though capers are low in calories, they are high in sodium because they are fermented in sea salt [41]. One tablespoon contains two kcal and 250 mg of sodium. However, rinsing under running water before using will remove some of the sodium in the caper (though not all, since they are brine) while maintaining their high flavour, and lowering the amount of extra salt. The caper's pungent nature offers an amazingly sharp and strong flavour to different sauces and condiments. Additionally, they can be used as a substitute for olives.

**Chickpeas (Garbanzos):** Data from PubMed Central and Chemistry Libretext shows that it contains folate with the coenzyme called THF (tetrahydrofolate), which is a key Coenzyme (COE) needed for the synthesis of amino acids and nucleic acids. For biochemical composition, half a cup of cooked chickpeas (82 g) is an excellent source of folate (35% DV), fibre (25% DV), and manganese (42% DV), and a good source of iron (13% DV), protein (15% DV), copper (15% DV), and magnesium (10% DV) [42]. For insights, an excellent source contains 20% and above of the recommended daily value (DV) based on a 2,000-kcal reference diet, while a good source contains 10%-19% of the recommended daily value. Chickpeas are also the key ingredient of hummus. Historically, a soup of black and regular chickpeas, lentils, fava beans, and whole wheat is an essential traditional cuisine in Puglia, Italy. Chickpea flour is used to prepare pancakes or crêpe called "farinata" or "Cecina" in Italy or "socca" in Cote d'Azur, France. Chickpeas have a stronger natural texture and flavour than many other beans to enjoy a Mediterranean-friendly snack, and you can roast cooked chickpeas and use salt on them like peanuts.

**Feta and yogurt:** The USDA nutritional information has illustrated that Feta and yogurt are rich source of calcium and promotes bone health [43]. The traditional Feta and yogurt are fermented, which makes them rich in probiotics. Feta and yogurt also provide extra protein to a mainly plant-based diet. Feta cheese is found in the classic Greek salad and is often used with stews. Original Greek Feta is prepared with goat or sheep's milk. Arguably, the people of Turkey introduced yogurt, which is more commonly utilized in the eastern Mediterranean, the old Ottoman Empire. Having yogurt with honey is a typical breakfast in Greece. However, American Feta is usually drier and slightly saltier than the imported one.

**Garlic:** It is a crucial ingredient in many Mediterranean dishes. How garlic is pronounced differs from area to area in the Mediterranean. Tzatziki, yogurt mixed with garlic, olive oil, red wine vinegar, cucumbers, and salt, is a typical sauce in many Eastern Mediterranean dishes. Aioli is produced by mixing garlic with eggs and olive oil. Biochemically, garlic's Sulfur compounds are creditworthy for its pungent odour and most of its health benefits, including anticancer, anti-inflammatory, and antioxidant effects. To fully enjoy the benefit of garlic, crush or chop it and leave it for 10-15 minutes before using it.

**Wine:** Alcohol intake was standard in the traditional Mediterranean diet, basically in moderate amounts and in the form of wine during meals. In the spirit of the ancient Greek term "symposium," Trichopoulou outlined. Wine intake is beneficial for health, especially red wine, which contains antioxidants called "polyphenols" and flavonoid resveratrol and can aid increase "HDL" cholesterol and reducing "LDL" cholesterol levels [44].

**Herbs:** They are rich in antioxidant and anti-inflammatory properties, especially polyphenols, and contribute effectively to the general dietary intake of flavanols and flavones in the traditional Greek dish. Each Mediterranean region has a unique flavour palette. Still, herbs and spices are highly essential in Mediterranean dishes. Adopt the Mediterranean style and add fresh herbs to salads to boost the antioxidant effects. Many classic herbs cultivated in North America usually grow wild along roads in the Mediterranean region.

## FOODS TO EAT IN THE MEDITERRANEAN DIET:

A major part of your diet should focus on the healthy foods contained in the Mediterranean diet pyramid. The diet is flexible. Choose foods from each group that you enjoy and aim to try new foods to discover new dishes and recipes. Several studies report the biochemical role of the Mediterranean diet is associated with improvements in memory, attention span, cognitive function, and processing speed in healthy older adults [18, 25, 45, 46, 47]. It is complex to tell which foods belong to the Mediterranean diet because of the variation in foods between these countries. The diet has been examined by many studies, which have found that the eating plan is rich in healthy plant-based foods and relatively low in meat and animal products. However, it is recommended to eat fish and seafood at least twice weekly. The Mediterranean diet is supplemented with regular physical activity, sharing meals with people, and reducing or managing stress levels.

Ideally, the Mediterranean diet emphasizes healthy eating foods such as:

**Whole grains:** Oats, corn, rye, barley, brown rice, buckwheat, whole wheat bread and pasta.

**Vegetables:** Broccoli, kale, spinach, tomatoes, onions, cauliflower, potatoes, carrots, Brussels sprouts, cucumbers, sweet potatoes, and turnips

**Nuts, seeds, and nut butter:** Walnuts, pumpkin seeds, macadamia nuts, cashews, almonds, hazelnuts, sunflower seeds, almond butter, and peanut butter.

**Fruits:** Bananas, oranges, figs, pears, strawberries, apples, grapes, dates, melons, and peaches.

**Fish and seafood:** Salmon, mackerel, trout, sardines, shrimp, oysters, tuna, clams, crab, and mussels.

**Legumes:** Peas, pulses, lentils, beans, peanuts, and chickpeas.

**Dairy:** yogurt, cheese, and milk.

**Poultry:** Turkey, chicken, and duck.

**Healthy fats:** Avocados, extra virgin olive oil, olives, and avocado oil.

**Eggs:** Quail, chicken, and duck eggs

**Herbs and spices:** Cinnamon, garlic, mint, rosemary, basil, sage, nutmeg, and pepper.

## FOODS TO LIMIT IN THE MEDITERRANEAN DIET:

It is not required to avoid these foods altogether, but it is essential to limit the amount and frequency of eating them. You are free to have them on a special occasion or occasionally. With that said, you should ensure to limit these processed foods and ingredients when following the Mediterranean diet:

**Refined grains:** Pasta, tortillas, white bread, chips, and crackers.

**Trans fats:** They are found in fried foods, margarine, and other processed foods

**Added sugar:** They are present in many foods, exceptionally high in ice cream, carbonated drinks, candies, syrup, table sugar, and baked goods

**Refined oils:** Soybean oil, grapeseed oil, canola oil, and cottonseed oil,

**Processed meat:** Processed sausages, pepperoni, deli meats, beef jerky, hot dogs, bologna, bacon, hot dogs, and sausage.

**Refined Carbohydrates and Sugar:** Cookies, cake, chips, doughnuts, pastries, crackers, soda, white bread, and white pasta.

**Highly processed foods:** Fast food, microwave popcorn, convenience meals, and granola bars.

**Red Meat:** Beef, bison, pork, and lamb.

**Beverages:** Water should be your best beverage on this eating plan. This diet also allows the intake of moderate amounts of red wine, about one glass daily. However, drinking wine is optional and should be avoided by many people, including pregnant women, individuals with challenges in drinking moderately, and people using certain medications that can interact with alcohol. Coffee and tea are other healthy beverages on this diet. Still, be cautious not to include lots of added sugar or cream in them. Limiting sugar-sweetened beverages like soda or sweet tea is crucial since they are primarily high in added sugar. Fruit juice may be taken in moderation, but you can opt for whole fruits to reap the benefit of fibre.

## FOODS TO EAT DAILY ON THE MEDITERRANEAN DIET:

**Whole Grains:** Brown rice, corn, whole wheat, quinoa, farro, amaranth, millet, and wild rice.

**Fruits:** Avocados, berries, apples, apricots, figs, grapes, dates, lemons, limes, pears, olives, oranges, and plums.

**Beans/Legumes:** Chickpeas, lentils, black-eyed peas, kidney beans, black beans, and navy beans.

**Vegetables:** Broccoli, carrots, cucumber, cauliflower, garlic, beets, herbs, kale, potatoes, onions, peppers, spinach, and tomatoes.

**Seeds:** Flaxseeds, pumpkin seeds, chia seeds, sunflower seeds, hemp seeds, and Extra Virgin Olive Oil

**Nuts:** Almonds, hazelnuts, pecans, cashews, pistachios, and walnuts.

**Healthy Beverages:** Water, coffee, tea, red wine – one drink daily for women and two drinks for men.

## FOODS TO EAT A FEW TIMES WEEKLY:

**Poultry:** Chicken and turkey.

**Dairy:** Greek yogurt, Parmesan cheese, feta cheese, kefir, goat cheese, and Eggs

## FOODS TO EAT ABOUT TWICE WEEKLY:

**Fish:** Salmon, tuna, sardines, and anchovies.

**Shellfish:** shrimp, mussels, clams, and crab.

## EATING OUT ON THE MEDITERRANEAN DIET:

One of the challenging parts of following a diet is knowing what to eat at restaurants, eateries, or social gatherings.

Fortunately, it is easy to sustain the Mediterranean diet while eating out. When eating out, incorporate many recommended foods and follow these few tips to help modify dishes. Here are some tips that can help you with your health and weight loss goals:

Consider or select fish or seafood as a main dish.

Ask if your dish can be cooked in extra virgin olive oil.

Opt for whole-grain bread with olive oil rather than butter.

Include vegetables in your order.

Choose water, unsweetened coffee/tea, or a glass of wine rather than soda.

Begin the meal with a salad and opt for vinaigrettes instead of creamy dressings. You can ask for a side of olive oil and vinegar and dress the salad yourself.

Order salad or fresh vegetables instead of French fries or refined grains

Opt for whole grains whenever you can.

Be picky with your protein. Check for the seafood options on the menu or choose dishes with plant-based protein.

When ordering meat, choose a smaller portion or divide it with someone because restaurants tend to over-serve.

For dessert, choose a bowl of fresh fruit. If it is unavailable and you want something sweet, divide the dessert with someone.

Social connection is an integral part of the Mediterranean diet, so becoming too focused on ordering the exact or appropriate food often defeats the socialization aspect.

CHAPTER TWO:

# HEALTH BENEFITS OF THE MEDITERRANEAN DIET

The biochemical basis of the traditional Mediterranean diet is that it is high in antioxidants, monounsaturated fatty acids, carotenoids, vitamin C, anthocyanins, tocopherols (vitamin E), polyphenols (mainly flavonoids), other vitamins and minerals, and dietary fibre [3]. The fat content of the diet is about 40% in Greece and 30% in Italy. Grains are whole or come in the form of fermented sourdough bread or pasta cooked (al dente), which reduces the glycemic index and the glycemic load. Furthermore, it is rich in phytochemicals, which have many anti-inflammatory benefits. The whole and minimally processed plant foods in the diet also provide prebiotic fibre, promoting and improving intestinal health. Several observational studies have found that following a

Mediterranean diet is associated with a reduction in the risk of many chronic diseases, including type 2 diabetes, cancer, Parkinson's disease, Alzheimer's disease, cardiovascular diseases, and untimely mortality [18, 25, 45, 46, 47].

The underlying biochemical role of the bioactive compounds of the Mediterranean diet has been associated with the following health benefits:

**It Supports Brain Health:** Research has found that consistent adherents of the Mediterranean Diet usually experience lower rates of dementia and neurodegenerative diseases and improved cognitive health [18, 48]. This can be linked to many dietary factors such as limited refined carbohydrate intake, high healthy fats and oils intake, and low saturated and trans fatty acids intake.

**It Reduces Risk of Cancer:** Not all forms of cancer are preventable, but certain lifestyle factors can help reduce their risk factors. Chronic inflammation is a primary contributor to the risk of cancer, and specific dietary factors in the Mediterranean diet can help reduce systemic inflammation levels [49, 50]. Studies have shown that high-fibre diets can reduce the risk of colon cancer, and many foods in the Mediterranean diet, including beans, vegetables, fruits, and whole grains, are excellent sources of fibre. Similarly, foods with high antioxidants may minimize inflammation, which may help reduce the risk of cancer [49]. Various other food types that are deeply-coloured fruits and vegetables like berries, kale, spinach, and sweet potatoes contain phytonutrients that have been found to decrease inflammation and therefore curb the risk of cancer.

**It Increases Lifespan:** The Mediterranean area is home to two Blue Zones, the regions with the reported highest number of centenarians and people living above the age of 100. The biochemical role of this diet reduces the risk of cancer, disease, and dementia, which naturally contribute to longevity and increase life [51]. Furthermore, the nutrient content of the foods in the Mediterranean Diet is a gateway to a long, healthy, and ailment-free life.

**It Supports Heart Health**: One of the most researched benefits of the Mediterranean Diet is its positive influence on heart health. Studies have found that people following this eating plan experience lower rates of dyslipidemia, heart disease, stroke, and hypertension [25, 26, 52]. The result of the studies has linked many of these benefits to a high intake of olive oil, legumes, fatty fish, beans, fresh herbs, and spices. However, many studies argue that these benefits are not related to a single food or nutrient. Instead, a combination of foods in the Mediterranean diet is what promotes heart health and provides cardioprotective effects.

## TAKEAWAY:

Studies have consistently found that the Mediterranean diet is beneficial in reducing the risk factors for diseases and mortality [53]. For example, a study of almost 26,000 women found that those who adopted this pattern of eating experienced 25% less risk of cardiovascular disease over 12 years.

The study examined various underlying mechanisms that may be responsible for this benefit and found that changes in blood sugar, inflammation, and body mass index were significant contributors.

CHAPTER THREE:

# MEAL PLANS AND SHOPPING LIST OF MEDITERRANEAN DIET

When planning for meals and groceries for the traditional Mediterranean diet, it is essential to remember that the diet focuses on plant foods, including fruits, nuts, vegetables, whole grains, seeds, and legumes, which are whole, minimally processed, seasonally fresh, and locally grown. In this diet, olive oil is the principal source of fat, cheese and yogurt are eaten daily in low or moderate amounts, fish and poultry are consumed in low or moderate amounts a few times weekly, red meat is consumed occasionally in small quantities, fresh fruit serves as dessert, sweets containing added sugars or honey are eaten only a few times weekly, and wine is consumed in low or moderate amounts, often with meals [3].

## SAMPLE MEAL PLAN FOR MEDITERRANEAN DIET:

There are numerous ways to incorporate the nutritious and toothsome foods of the Mediterranean diet into your daily meals. Below is an easy way to begin.

**Breakfast:**

Plain Greek yogurt topped with nuts and fresh berries.

Whole-grain bread topped with a small number of fresh tomato slices, and low-fat cheese and drizzled with a little extra virgin olive oil

Vegetable omelet prepared with spinach, mushrooms, and onions cooked in olive oil with crusty whole-grain bread.

This sample meal plan contains approximately 2000 calories, which is the recommended intake for an average human. However, if you have higher calorie needs, you can include an additional snack or two. Similarly, you can remove a snack if you have lower-calorie needs. Consult with a registered dietitian and healthcare provider if you have more specific nutritional needs or would need help in designing meal plans that are suitable for your weight loss goals.

# 1-DAY SAMPLE MEAL MENU FOR MEDITERRANEAN DIET:

**Breakfast:**

Try one cup of cooked steel-cut oats mixed with two tablespoons of chopped walnuts, ¾ cup of fresh or frozen blueberries, and a sprinkle of cinnamon.

**Snack:**

¼ cup of any type of nuts

**Lunch:**

Try beans and rice. In a medium pot, heat one tablespoon of olive oil, add and sauté ½ chopped onion, one teaspoon of cumin, and one teaspoon of garlic powder until the onion is softened. After that, mix in 1 cup of canned beans, drain and rinse. Serve the bean mixture over 1 cup of cooked brown rice.

2 cups of salad (cucumbers, or mixed greens, or cucumbers, bell peppers) with dressing (mix two tablespoons of olive oil, one tablespoon of lemon juice or vinegar, ½ teaspoon of garlic powder, ½ teaspoon of Dijon mustard, ¼ teaspoon of black pepper)

**Snack:**

One medium orange

**Dinner:**

One cup of chopped steamed cauliflower

Three ounces of baked salmon brushed with the same salad dressing used at lunch

One medium baked sweet potato with one tablespoon of soft margarine

**Snack:**

1 ounce of 75% dark chocolate

# 7-DAY SAMPLE MEAL MENU FOR MEDITERRANEAN DIET:

The following is a sample menu for a week of dishes to begin with the Mediterranean diet. You can modify the portions and food choices based on your requirements, tastes, preferences, and weight loss goals. Moreover, you can also add snacks as desired.

**Day 1:**

**Breakfast:** Greek yogurt with chia seeds and strawberries.

**Lunch:** Whole-grain sandwich with hummus and veggies.

**Dinner:** Tuna salad with olive oil, greens, and fruit salad.

**Day 2:**

**Breakfast:** Bowl of oatmeal with blueberries.

**Lunch:** Caprese zucchini noodles with mozzarella, olive oil, cherry tomatoes, and balsamic vinegar

**Dinner:** Salad with tomatoes, cucumbers, olives, farro, grilled chicken, and feta cheese.

**Day 3:**

**Breakfast:** An omelet with tomatoes, mushrooms, and onions.

**Lunch:** Whole-grain sandwich with cheese and fresh veggies.

**Dinner:** A plate of Mediterranean lasagna.

## Day 4:

**Breakfast:** Yoghurt with nuts and sliced fruit.

**Lunch:** Quinoa salad with chickpeas.

**Dinner:** Broiled salmon with brown rice and veggies.

## Day 5:

**Breakfast:** Eggs and sautéed veggies with whole-wheat toast.

**Lunch:** Stuffed zucchini boats with pesto, tomatoes, turkey sausage, bell peppers, and cheese.

**Dinner:** Grilled lamb with baked potato and salad.

## Day 6:

**Breakfast:** Oatmeal with nuts, raisins, and apple slices.

**Lunch:** Whole-grain sandwich with veggies.

**Dinner:** Mediterranean pizza made with whole-wheat pita bread and topped with veggies, cheese, and olives.

## Day 7:

**Breakfast:** An omelette with vegetables and olives

**Lunch:** Falafel bowl with Feta, tomatoes, hummus, onions, and rice.

**Dinner:** Grilled chicken with veggies, sweet potato fries, and fresh fruit.

# HEALTHY SHOPPING LIST FOR MEDITERRANEAN DIET:

Having a handy amount of healthy pantry staples and fridge essentials makes it easier to follow and sustain a diet, lose weight quickly, and achieve your health goals. The list might differ for each person depending on budget, cultural background, dietary needs, or cooking skills. Still, this is not a call for you to limit your shopping list to only the food groups listed here; instead, they are essentials to have handy.

# HEALTHY PANTRY STAPLES LIST:

**Vegetables:** Some veggies should be stored in a pantry or the counter. Onions and garlic are essential ingredients to add and improve flavour to your meals. Any variety of potatoes is necessary and should be made handy.

**Grains:** Add whole grains to your pantry, since they are an excellent source of fibre, phytochemicals, minerals, vitamins, and healthy fats than refined grains. Stock your pantry with whole-grain pasta, brown rice, bean or lentil pasta, oats, and classic grains like quinoa and farro.

**Nuts & Seeds:** They add a crunchy and creamy texture to recipes and provide healthy fats and proteins. Nuts and seeds are excellent for salads, baked goods, and healthy snacks. For biochemical relevance, walnuts are significantly high in heart-healthy omega-3 fatty acids. However, all varieties of nuts are considered beneficial in this diet. Ensure to store your walnuts and ground flaxseeds in the refrigerator for extended shelf life.

**Dried Fruit:** Like nuts and seeds, dried fruits are an excellent addition to salads and baked goods. Search for no-added-sugar varieties, though some fruits like cranberries need the sugar. Try integrating dried fruit with nuts and seeds to enjoy a healthy trail mix.

**Oils:** It is essential to have a variety of oils at hand since they serve different purposes. Dieticians recommend extra virgin olive oil as an essential oil because it is high in monounsaturated fats and polyphenols and protects the body against cancer, heart disease, etc. [33]. Olive oil is a crucial ingredient in the Mediterranean Diet for its many health benefits and biochemical roles [32]. For easy tips, reserve the expensive bottles of oils for salad dressings and finishing, and use the cost-effective ones for sautéing and roasting since the "smoke point" is not actually a life-threatening issue. Avocado and canola oil are good and healthy options, too, and serve as neutrally flavoured alternatives for roasting and baking. Coconut oil can be a healthy vegan butter alternative, and sesame oil is a flavourful addition to Asian dishes. To save the oil from separating, ensure to stir before refrigerating. Research has found that all varieties of oil are healthy, do well to choose your favourite.

**Spices & Dried Herbs:** They provide flavourful and nutritional benefits. They are essential for this diet. Turmeric has anti-inflammatory effects, and ginger improves digestion. Hence, it is crucial to keep the following herbs and spices handy:

*Chili Powder*

*Ginger*

*Black Pepper*

*Cinnamon*

*Paprika*

*Oregano*

*Italian Seasoning*

*Thyme*

*Cumin*

*Garlic Powder*

Additionally, you can explore and add new spices and herbs to your diet.

**Salt:** Most people must reduce their salt intake to avoid high blood pressure, but it is crucial for making palatable food. Experts recommend using kosher salt as it's easy to see and determine the quantity you're using. Sea salt is another healthy alternative with a more robust flavour that allows you to use less of it.

**Dried and/or Canned Beans:** Beans are nutritious, extremely healthy, and affordable staple food in several countries that improve health and promote longevity. They are great sources of plant-based protein and an excellent source of fibre. Keep a variety of beans handy, though canned beans are convenient (buy low-sodium varieties) and dried beans are more affordable. Nevertheless, both offer similar health benefits.

**Canned Tomatoes:** Canned tomatoes are an essential and multi-purpose ingredient of food that should be kept handy for different uses, including whole or crushed, diced, pureed, fire-roasted, and paste. You can use them for making pasta dishes, homemade marinara, curries, tomato-based sauces, beans, and soups. Canned tomatoes are rich in phytonutrient lycopene than fresh tomatoes, and a high intake of phytonutrients may help reduce the risk of certain cancers.

**Stock or Broth:** They add flavour to sauces, rice, beans, and soups and should be kept handy. Choose chicken or vegetable stock, and carefully examine sodium before purchasing. It is advisable to buy the no-added-salt varieties to limit the amount of salt in the cuisine and season meals to your taste.

**Vinegar:** They are essential for making dressings. Apple cider, balsamic, and red wine vinegar are crucial to have handy. Use balsamic vinegar for a sweeter and more complex flavour.

**Condiments:** They are flavour enhancers and can also be used alone on or for many sauces. Dieticians recommend storing hot sauce, maple syrup, honey, reduced-sodium soy sauce, or tamari in your pantry. Likewise, fruit preserves, sauces, mustards, hummus, and curry paste. You should include tahini in your grocery list and store it in the refrigerator after mixing.

**Natural Cheese:** Choose block or shredded cheese. They are excellent for making sandwiches, homemade pizza, quesadillas, and garnishing soups, salads, and Italian dishes. Stronger cheeses like Feta, goat, or blue are ideal choices since a small amount can significantly improve the flavours of a dish.

**Yogurt and/or Kefir:** They provide all the probiotics you will need without a supplement. Kefir is ideal for smoothies, and yogurt can be added to dressings, sweet or savoury dips, or sauces.

**Seafood and fish:** This is one of the best ways to eat adequate omega-3 fatty acids. Fish is fish and comes in handy for a quick weeknight dinner.

**Eggs:** Eggs are healthy sources of protein and essential nutrients.

CHAPTER FOUR:

# THE MEDITERRANEAN DIET RECIPES

For years, the Mediterranean culture has been investigated and adopted as a source of inspiration for healthy eating and living. The Mediterranean diet focuses on fruits, vegetables, fish, and healthy fats that are whole and minimally processed. Following a style of eating obtainable in countries like Greece, Italy, Spain, and Turkey s been shown to reduce the risk of chronic diseases due to the biochemical role of its key ingredients[54]. Do you want some help with recipes for breakfast, lunch, dinner, or dessert? This chapter has a collection of recipes you can choose from to enjoy Mediterranean eating. Enjoy your way to healthy weight loss!

## 1. Greek-Style Zucchini Blossoms Stuffed with Bulgur:

This Chickpea and Aubergine warm salad has fresh and filling ingredients with health-promoting effects. Bulgur wheat is common in dishes around the Middle East and serves as a popular grain in Greek meals. This tasty and delightful stuffed-zucchini recipe can be served as a side dish or a vegan main dish. The good thing is that it is also gluten-free.

**Serves:** 4 as a side

**Ingredients:**

- One tin of chickpeas, well-drained
- Four tablespoons of extra-virgin olive oil
- One large aubergine (eggplant), cut into 2cm cubes
- One teaspoon of paprika
- One garlic clove, skin on and bashed with the back of a knife
- Salt and pepper for seasoning
- Parsley leaves and nasturtium to spread on top

**Instruction:**

1. Heat the oil in a large, non-stick frying pan, add garlic, and cook to absorb its scent for 1 minute.
2. Add the aubergine, stir thoroughly until it is well-coated with the oil, then turn down the heat to medium-low, cover the frying pan with a lid and allow the hot oil and steam to gently cook the vegetables for 15 minutes. Ensure to stir occasionally.
3. When the aubergines are soft and slightly caramelized, add chickpeas and paprika, stir thoroughly and cook uncovered over medium heat for 4-5 minutes. Toast in salt and adjust accordingly to taste.
4. Serve it warm and topped with parsley, nasturtium leaves, and ground black pepper.

## 2. Calabrian Swordfish with Capers (Pesce Spada con capperi alla calabrese):

Swordfish is widely accepted for its mild taste and meaty texture. The large size of large fish size ensures that it is primarily sold in large, boneless steaks that promote a freewheeling eating experience. Many people who are not flighty about other types of fish may enjoy this recipe. Swordfish is a popular fish in the southern-most region of Italy, especially Sicily, which is rightly famous for its swordfish cuisines like Pesce Spada con salmoriglio (swordfish with pasta). Additionally, cities like Calabria have tasty swordfish cuisines too. This swordfish with capers can be cooked in just a few minutes. This recipe is easy-to-prepare and more delicious, the sauce resonates with Sicily's salmoriglio, but it is cooked instead of raw.

**Serves:** 4-6

**Ingredients:**

- Olive oil
- One swordfish steak per person

- 1-2 garlic cloves, peeled and slightly crushed (optional)
- Salt.

*For the sauce:*

- One freshly squeezed lemon juice
- A pinch of oregano
- A few sprigs of parsley, finely minced
- A handful of capers
- A pinch of red pepper flakes (optional)

**Instructions:**

1. Over moderate heat, sauté the swordfish steaks in olive oil for about three minutes on each side until they become lightly brown, and season them to taste as they cook.
2. Remove the steaks from the skillet and allow them to become warm. If you use garlic, add it to the skillet with the swordfish and remove it when the steaks are done.
3. Add the sauce ingredients to the skillet, let it simmer, and allow them to reduce for only a minute or two.
4. Spread the swordfish steaks with the sauce and serve immediately.

## 3. Lentil Soup with Kale:

This delicious recipe is tasty with kale but may be easily made with Swiss chard or spinach, too if they are fresh. Traditional Mediterranean cooking seldom includes convenience foods such as frozen or canned vegetables.

### Ingredients:

- Two garlic cloves finely chopped
- One 1/2 cup of canned chopped tomatoes
- Three cups of water or vegetable stock
- Three cups of trimmed chopped fresh kale
- Two bar leaves
- One large red onion finely chopped
- 2 – 3 tablespoons Vrisi 36 Greek balsamic vinegar
- 1/3 cup of Extra virgin Greek olive oil or more for drizzling
- One pound of small brown or green lentils rinsed and drained
- One dried chile pepper (optional)
- Salt and pepper to taste

**Instructions:**

- In a large pot over medium heat, heat the olive oil and wilt the onions, occasionally stirring, for 7 – 8 minutes.
- Add the garlic and stir for a minute until it softens; add the lentils and stir to coat in the olive oil.
- Add the tomatoes, chile pepper (optional), bay leaf, and tomatoes. Pour in the water or stock, boil it at medium heat and reduce to a simmer. Add water or stock, if necessary, to ensure an optimal covering of liquid by two inches. Allow it to simmer covered for 45 – 50 minutes, or until the lentils become soft but al dente.
- Stir in the chopped kale and season it with salt and pepper to taste. Add more water if needed. Simmer the soup for another 10 minutes or until the kale becomes tender.
- Stir in the balsamic and adjust the seasoning with salt and pepper to taste as desired.
- Serve in personal bowls and drizzle at least one tablespoon of Vrisi 36 Bold olive oil in each serving.

## 4. Grilled fish in the saffron sauce:

This delightful summer dish is surprisingly easy to prepare. This Lebanese recipe is made with whole fish, but you can also swap it with larger fillets like swordfish.

**Servings:** 4

**Preparation Time:** 5 minutes

**Cook Time:** 10 minutes

**Ingredients:**

- Four fishes (any type) (whole can be swapped with fillets, such as catfish or swordfish)
- One large lemon or lime quartered
- 1/2 cup of vegetable oil (walnut oil is acceptable too)
- 1/2 cup tomato sauce or 1 tbsp tomato paste or ketchup
- One pinch of saffron in filaments soaked in 1/4 cup of hot water for 10 minutes beforehand
- One teaspoon of sea salt to taste
- 1/2 teaspoon of white pepper can be swapped with other spices like cumin or sumac

**Instructions:**

1. Heat the grill till it becomes very hot, season the fish, and brush it with oil. Brush the grill with oil before grilling the fish to prevent it from sticking.
2. Grill the fish for three minutes on each side and brush it with the sauce every 15 seconds.
3. Serve it hot with lemon or lime quarters.
4. In a small bowl, blend all the sauce ingredients, and add more tomato sauce or spices to taste. Use a brush to use when coating the fish with the sauce.

# HEALTHY MEDITERRANEAN BREAKFAST CHOICES:

Breakfast accelerates your metabolism, help you burn calories, and stays energized during the day. These are just a few of the many reasons it is the day's most important meal. The Mediterranean diet is a great and healthy choice for losing weight in a healthy manner. However, knowing how to create a healthy breakfast and sticking to the key principles of the diet can be challenging. Don't lose hope and figure out the best recipes, which include trying out newer meals depending on your cravings. Below is a list of healthy breakfast recipes on the Mediterranean diet to choose from:

**i. Strawberry-Thyme Millet Bowl:** Begin your day off with an energizing bowl of millet to stay filled for a long duration, eat less, and burn more calories. Roasting strawberries with herbs and honey gives a delicious, nutritious, and savoury feeling. Having millet in the morning provides adequate nutrition to keep you satiated and focused during the day.

**ii. Instant Pot Sunday Pot Roast:** This is easy to prepare, nutritious, and contains 45 grams of protein and 4 grams of carbs which is crucial for weight loss and general health.

**iii. Blueberry Smoothie Bowl:** This recipe includes fresh fruits, almond butter, and more to provide you with the protein, vitamins, healthy fats, minerals, and fibre necessary to stay healthy and lose weight. This is more than just another bowl of breakfast.

**iv. Slow Cooker Everything Chicken:** This recipe contains 29 grams of protein and 2 grams of carbs, making it healthy, filling, and sustainable. An easy pick for accelerating weight loss.

**v. Cauliflower "Tabbouleh":** This is not a traditional breakfast dish, but a blend of cauliflower-based tabbouleh makes it nutritious and a vegetable-based approach to beginning the day and staying energized. The lesser you eat, the lesser the calories consumed.

**vi. 3-Ingredient Tender Broiled Salmon:** These healthy recipes contain 34 grams of protein and 1 gram of carb, which screams healthy and is crucial for weight loss.

**vii. Scrambled Egg Tacos:** Tacos are not from the Mediterranean, but losing weight includes eating black beans and spinach for the intake of extra protein and fibre necessary for curbing cravings, eating less, staying full, and promoting overall health. You will love the flavours of early morning tacos, and it is easier to prepare in just 15 minutes.

**viii. Snow Pea and Ricotta Toasts:** This recipe, like the Mediterranean diet, focuses on vegetable intake. Will this help you to lose weight and stay healthy? Of course! Snow peas provide an adequate amount of fibre and folate, while ricotta and honey provide the sweetness that keeps you satisfied.

**ix. Whipped Feta and Watermelon Radishes Toast:** This recipe is breakfast-worthy, and watermelon radishes and sprouts usher a breath of freshness to your morning. You can combine them with whipped creamy Feta and a hunky slice of sourdough to have a delightful, yummy, and delicious plate.

**x. Grain Bowl with Sautéed Spinach:** This recipe is dairy-free and promotes health and weight loss. For a light yet filling breakfast, pair leftover grains, avocado, tomato, and a fried egg.

**xi. Tomato Toasts with Mint yogurt and Sumac Vinaigrette:** This recipe offers some tasty toasts with classic Greek yogurt and adds taste with lemon, mint, and scallions. For a perfect breakfast, top this recipe with juicy tomatoes and a delicate dressing. Adding a hard-boiled egg on the side will make it a more nutritious Mediterranean breakfast in a few minutes.

**xii. Sautéed Dandelion Toast:** This recipe uses nutrient-dense greens and onions to make this toast, and topping whole-grain with Feta, lemon juice, and Greek yogurt makes it fill and highly satisfying.

## MEDITERRANEAN DIET LUNCH:

The Mediterranean diet is one of the healthiest eating plans to follow in a bid to lose weight and maintain health. These lunch choices make it delicious, highly nutritious, easy to follow and help keep you filled throughout the day.

**i. Quinoa Salad with Feta, Olives & Tomatoes:** This recipe draws inspiration from a Greek salad which makes it filling and flavourful. Broiling the olives with other vegetables improves the flavour and adds a smoky feeling, while garnishing with basil perfects the dish.

**ii. Super Easy Pork Tenderloin with Garlic and Rosemary:** This recipe contains 35 grams of protein and no carbs, which makes it health friendly and an excellent tool for weight loss.

**iii. Mediterranean Pasta Salad:** It may be hard to imagine using hummus as a pasta sauce, but the creamy dip is the perfect setting for the enhanced flavours of this healthy pasta salad inspired by the Mediterranean.

**iv. Baked Falafel Sandwiches:** This street-style falafel sandwich is sourish, healthy, and full of herbs. The falafel becomes nice and crispy in the oven, while the veggies make it simple and fresh. Prepare the tahini sauce beforehand for easy preparation. You can wrap the sandwich in foil to make it easier to carry for eating wherever you go.

**v. Chia seeds:** This healthy and weight-loss-promoting recipe contains five grams of protein and 12 grams of carbs per serving (one ounce), making it nutritious and sustainable.

**vi. Tomato, Cucumber & White-Bean Salad with Basil Vinaigrette:** This no-cook bean salad recipe is a delicious blend of summer's best cherry or grape tomatoes and juicy cucumbers for making lunch or light dinner. Fresh basil blends easily with a vinaigrette recipe that dresses up this simple to make salad into a fantastic dish.

**vii. Mediterranean Chickpea Quinoa Bowl:** This recipe is made with vegetarian grain and plenty of plant-based protein. You can easily whip up a batch of these Mediterranean meals and store them in flasks or containers with lids to stock in the fridge for easy, healthy, and grab & go lunch throughout the week.

**viii. 5-Ingredient Vegan "Chicken" Salad Recipe:** This recipe contains 11 grams of protein and six grams of carbs which is ideal for losing weight faster and healthier.

**ix. Salmon Rice Bowl:** This tasty bowl can be chosen for a filling and delightful lunch or dinner. Using healthy ingredients like heart-healthy salmon, instant brown rice, and some crunchy veggies, you can prepare this filling and flavourful meal in just 25 minutes. You can also replace brown rice with cauliflower rice to cut down on carbohydrates.

**x. Baked Tofu Chunks with Star Anise Marinade:** This recipe is healthy, tasty, easy to prepare, and contains 19 grams of protein and eight grams of carbs.

**xi. Mason Jar Power Salad with Chickpeas & Tuna:** This potent salad will keep you filled and energized for hours because of its 26 grams of protein and eight grams of fibre content. You can toss the dressing and kale and allow it to stand in the jar, but soften it enough to avoid a need to massage or cook it to become tender.

**xii. Maple Glazed Tempeh:** This recipe is healthy and nutritious and contains 31 grams of protein and 15 grams of carbs per serving which is 6 ounces). This is a delightful choice to accelerate your weight loss journey.

## MEDITERRANEAN DIET DINNER:

These are some healthy and weight-loss-promoting dinner options on the Mediterranean diet:

**i. Balsamic Glazed Whole Roasted Cauliflower:** This recipe is healthy and contains ten grams of carbs and 3 grams of protein.

**ii. Mediterranean Quinoa Bowls with Roasted Red Pepper Sauce:** This is a low-carb, high-protein, and highly filling meal.

**iii. 3-Ingredient Spicy Roasted Broccoli:** It is healthy and contains one gram of carb and 1 gram of protein.

**iv. Baked Chicken and Ricotta Meatballs:** When you have leftover meatballs, warm them in broth and toss them in healthy greens to make this quick soup.

**v. Mediterranean Couscous with Tuna and Pepperoncini:** This recipe is easy to prepare and ready in just 15 minutes.

**vi. Mozzarella, Basil & Zucchini Frittata:** This vegetable-rich frittata recipe is one of the easiest and quickest meals to prepare. It can be consumed during breakfast or served at lunch or dinner with a tossed salad and a slice of crusty baguette that is olive oil drizzled.

**vii. Spicy Broiled Green Beans:** This recipe contains nine grams of carbs and two grams of protein. It promotes weight loss and supports overall health.

**viii. Healthy Balsamic Chicken Skillet:** This recipe is colorful and serves as the perfect dish for any dinner of the week.

**ix. One-Skillet Greek Sun-Dried Tomato Chicken and Farro:** This recipe is prepared with pan-seared chicken, fresh oregano, lemon dill, garlic, and paprika, and cooked with farro, olives, sun-dried tomatoes.

**x. Dijon Roasted Garlic Asparagus:** This dish is healthy and has only six grams of carbs and three grams of protein.

**xi. Greek Wedge Salad:** This is a classic dish that is easy to prepare and promotes weight loss.

## MEDITERRANEAN DIET DESSERT AND SUGAR:

There are no foods that are entirely off-limits or restricted in the Mediterranean diet, including dessert. This popular eating plan incorporates healthy fats, veggies, fruits, nuts, and low-fat dairy, which means what you eat doesn't have to taste like "diet food."

**i. Peaches and Cream Ice Pops:** This is a healthy dessert and treat. You can reduce the amount of sugar while roasting the peaches. If the fruit is ripe and in its season, it should be tasty enough not to affect the taste.

**ii. Avocado Chocolate Mousse:** This rich, creamy, and chocolate-filled treat is plant-based and dairy-free because of the avocado. Don't panic, and it does not taste like a vegetable.

**iii. 1-Ingredient Watermelon Sorbet:** This is easy to make dessert. The seeded watermelons have more flavour. Still, if you can't deal with it, simply use a seedless melon.

**iv. Easy 5-Ingredient Garlic Herb Sauteed Mushrooms:** This contains five grams of carbs and four grams of protein which makes it healthy and easy to lose weight with.

**v. Orange Flower Olive Oil Cake:** This cake contains sugar, but it is also prepared with olive oil instead of butter, making it healthy for the heart. Apart from olive oil being a staple on the Mediterranean diet, it keeps the cake highly moist for days.

**vi. 5-Minute Greek Yoghurt Pumpkin Parfait:** This thick, nutritious, and creamy spiced pumpkin yogurt is a healthy substitute for ice cream. These parfaits can be topped with dark chocolate chips, toasted nuts, both, and anything beneficial.

**vii. Baked Pears with Maple Syrup and Almond Crumble:** To make this, you can use any type of pear, but Bosc and Anjou pears will best maintain shape in the oven. Additionally, this dessert tastes yummy with apples.

**viii. Aran Goyoaga's Peanut Butter–Banana Cookies:** This cookie is rich in healthy and nutritious ingredients like banana and nut butter.

**ix. No-Bake, Gluten-Free Rose Petal Brownies:** This treat is sugar-free and healthy. Adding rose petals to it is optional, but the cocoa-maple glaze is a necessity.

**x. Raw Vegan Brownies Bites:** This treat is a fantastic way to incorporate chocolate into your diet and enjoy dates.

## CHAPTER FIVE:

# THE MEDITERRANEAN DIET PROMOTES CONSISTENCY AS A LIFESTYLE

For most people, the word "diet" is associated with calorie counting, food restrictions, and other regimental registers. However, the Mediterranean diet is the antithesis of that and is full of foods commonly eaten in Greece, Italy, Turkey, Spain, Israel, and other regions of the Middle East. This diet is a lifestyle practice that focuses on olive oil, whole grains, fruits, vegetables, low-fat dairy, beans, nuts, fish, healthy fats, etc. Following this diet for three months or more has been scientifically proven to promote weight loss, improve mental acuity, support heart health, and improve general health [48, 54, 55].

The Mediterranean diet is more of a lifestyle than a diet because the goal of this diet includes socializing, promoting overall health, and reducing the manmade impact on the environment by reducing the intake of red meat, fish, dairy, and packaged foods [7]. A traditional Mediterranean diet may still include these products in smaller or moderate amounts while focusing on whole and minimally processed plant foods. This diet is sustainable and an excellent dietary choice for a person's general health because it doesn't include counting calories or tracking macronutrients (carbohydrates, protein, fat) on the Mediterranean diet.

The Mediterranean Diet is nutritionally rich and is considered an anti-inflammatory diet [45]. This lifestyle practice is more sustainable than most diets because it is an eating plan and encourages physical activity and social interaction, which are an integral part of healthy living. This eating pattern is adopted to improve general health and quality of living through making changes to diet, exercise routines, social habits, and self-preservation approaches. Therefore, the Mediterranean Diet is beyond just an eating pattern because engaging in regular physical activity and sharing meals with family, colleagues, and friends are essential to the Mediterranean Diet pyramid [21]. Doing these can significantly affect your mood and mental health and help you have a deep and sincere appreciation for the beauty of healthy eating and delicious foods.

# CONCLUSION

The Mediterranean diet is based on the traditional dishes of people living by the Mediterranean Sea, such as Greece, Italy, Spain, Turkey, and Israel. The diet typically consists of whole and minimally processed fruits, seafood, vegetables, beans, nuts, olive oil, beans, dairy, nuts, herbs, spices, whole grains, and room for a glass or two of red wine. Some foods, like animal proteins, are eaten in smaller quantities and in moderation. Fish and seafood are the preferred animal protein in this diet.

The Mediterranean diet is proposed as a healthy and well-balanced diet that can improve health, boost vitality, fight many chronic diseases, and prevent health conditions by reducing cholesterol. The efficacy of this diet against heart diseases, cognitive decline, and type 2 diabetes is well documented. The principles behind the Mediterranean diet are simple and focus on eating a more plant-based diet and relatively less meat and other animal products. It could be a significant dietary and lifestyle change for some people. The Mediterranean diet is an affordable way to eat foods that can help you live healthier and longer. Hence, for health, economic and environmental reasons, anyone can follow the Mediterranean diet, which is not restrictive and can be sustained for extended periods.

Dieticians have asserted that combining the many components of the Mediterranean diet is more imperative in losing weight and maintaining health than eating one food in isolation. Trichopoulou cited a piece of significant evidence for a synergy between the components of the Mediterranean diet to provide many vitamins, minerals, and phytochemicals.

## HOW TO FOLLOW THE MEDITERRANEAN DIET?

- **Eat:** Fruits, nuts, vegetables, seeds, potatoes, legumes, whole grains, herbs, seafood, spices, fish, and extra virgin olive oil.
- **Eat in moderation:** Eggs, cheese, poultry, and yogurt

- **Eat rarely:** Added sugars, refined grains, red meat, refined oils, sugar-sweetened beverages, processed meat, and other highly processed foods

*-- Prince N. Agbedanu*

# REFERENCES

1 Zhang, X.M., et al., *Comment on "global prevalence of sarcopenic obesity in older adults: A systematic review and meta-analysis".* Clin Nutr, 2022. **41**(6): p. 1451-1453.

2 Castro-Quezada, I., B. Roman-Vinas, and L. Serra-Majem, *The Mediterranean diet and nutritional adequacy: a review.* Nutrients, 2014. **6**(1): p. 231-48.

3 Schwingshackl, L., J. Morze, and G. Hoffmann, *Mediterranean diet and health status: Active ingredients and pharmacological mechanisms.* Br J Pharmacol, 2020. **177**(6): p. 1241-1257.

4 Beltran Sanahuja, A., et al., *Influence of Cooking and Ingredients on the Antioxidant Activity, Phenolic Content and Volatile Profile of Different Variants of the Mediterranean Typical Tomato Sofrito.* Antioxidants (Basel), 2019. **8**(11).

5 Bakaloudis, D.E., et al., *Diet composition and feeding strategies of the stone marten (Martes foina) in a typical Mediterranean ecosystem.* ScientificWorldJournal, 2012. **2012**: p. 163920.

6 Mistretta, A., et al., *Mediterranean diet adherence and body composition among Southern Italian adolescents.* Obes Res Clin Pract, 2017. **11**(2): p. 215-226.

7 Castaldi, S., et al., *The positive climate impact of the Mediterranean diet and current divergence of Mediterranean countries towards less climate sustainable food consumption patterns.* Sci Rep, 2022. **12**(1): p. 8847.

8 Baudet, M.F., et al., *Effects of three dietary fats on plasma lipids and lipoproteins in fasting and post-prandial humans after a short-term diet.* Lipids, 1980. **15**(4): p. 216-23.

9   Alhashemi, M., et al., *Prevalence of obesity and its association with fast-food consumption and physical activity: A cross-sectional study and review of medical students' obesity rate.* Ann Med Surg (Lond), 2022. **79**: p. 104007.

10  Asselin, G., et al., *Fasting and postprandial lipid response to the consumption of modified milk fats by guinea pigs.* Lipids, 2004. **39**(10): p. 985-92.

11  Liu, Y., et al., *Post-exercise Effects and Long-Term Training Adaptations of Hormone Sensitive Lipase Lipolysis Induced by High-Intensity Interval Training in Adipose Tissue of Mice.* Front Physiol, 2020. **11**: p. 535722.

12  Nagy, E., et al., *The effects of exercise capacity and sedentary lifestyle on haemostasis among middle-aged women with coronary heart disease.* Thromb Haemost, 2008. **100**(5): p. 899-904.

13  Agrawal, P., et al., *Effects of sedentary lifestyle and dietary habits on body mass index change among adult women in India: findings from a follow-up study.* Ecol Food Nutr, 2013. **52**(5): p. 387-406.

14  Xi, B., et al., *Association between common polymorphism near the MC4R gene and obesity risk: a systematic review and meta-analysis.* PLoS One, 2012. **7**(9): p. e45731.

15  Perakakis, N., O.M. Farr, and C.S. Mantzoros, *Leptin in Leanness and Obesity: JACC State-of-the-Art Review.* J Am Coll Cardiol, 2021. **77**(6): p. 745-760.

16  Salum, K.C.R., et al., *When Leptin Is Not There: A Review of What Nonsyndromic Monogenic Obesity Cases Tell Us and the Benefits of Exogenous Leptin.* Front Endocrinol (Lausanne), 2021. **12**: p. 722441.

17  Martinez-Lacoba, R., et al., *Mediterranean diet and health outcomes: a systematic meta-review.* Eur J Public Health, 2018. **28**(5): p. 955-961.

18  Fu, J., et al., *Association between the mediterranean diet and cognitive health among healthy adults: A systematic review and meta-analysis.* Front Nutr, 2022. **9**: p. 946361.

19   Buckland, G., A. Bach, and L. Serra-Majem, *Obesity and the Mediterranean diet: a systematic review of observational and intervention studies.* Obes Rev, 2008. **9**(6): p. 582-93.

20   Sarsangi, P., et al., *Association between Adherence to the Mediterranean Diet and Risk of Type 2 Diabetes: An Updated Systematic Review and Dose-Response Meta-Analysis of Prospective Cohort Studies.* Adv Nutr, 2022.

21   Bach-Faig, A., et al., *Mediterranean diet pyramid today. Science and cultural updates.* Public Health Nutr, 2011. **14**(12A): p. 2274-84.

22   D'Alessandro, A. and G. De Pergola, *Mediterranean diet pyramid: a proposal for Italian people.* Nutrients, 2014. **6**(10): p. 4302-16.

23   Vitiello, V., et al., *The New Modern Mediterranean Diet Italian Pyramid.* Ann Ig, 2016. **28**(3): p. 179-86.

24   Karamanos, B., et al., *Nutritional habits in the Mediterranean Basin. The macronutrient composition of diet and its relation with the traditional Mediterranean diet. Multi-centre study of the Mediterranean Group for the Study of Diabetes (MGSD).* Eur J Clin Nutr, 2002. **56**(10): p. 983-91.

25   Filippou, C.D., et al., *Mediterranean diet and blood pressure reduction in adults with and without hypertension: A systematic review and meta-analysis of randomized controlled trials.* Clin Nutr, 2021. **40**(5): p. 3191-3200.

26   Billingsley, H.E. and S. Carbone, *The antioxidant potential of the Mediterranean diet in patients at high cardiovascular risk: an in-depth review of the PREDIMED.* Nutr Diabetes, 2018. **8**(1): p. 13.

27   Sanchez-Sanchez, M.L., et al., *Mediterranean diet and health: A systematic review of epidemiological studies and intervention trials.* Maturitas, 2020. **136**: p. 25-37.

28   Serra-Majem, L., et al., *Updating the Mediterranean Diet Pyramid towards Sustainability: Focus on Environmental Concerns.* Int J Environ Res Public Health, 2020. **17**(23).

29   D'Alessandro, A., L. Lampignano, and G. De Pergola, *Mediterranean Diet Pyramid: A Proposal for Italian People. A*

Systematic Review of Prospective Studies to Derive Serving Sizes. Nutrients, 2019. **11**(6).

30. Diolintzi, A., D.B. Panagiotakos, and L.S. Sidossis, *From Mediterranean diet to Mediterranean lifestyle: a narrative review.* Public Health Nutr, 2019. **22**(14): p. 2703-2713.

31. Mayer, B., et al., *Effects of an onion-olive oil maceration product containing essential ingredients of the Mediterranean diet on blood pressure and blood fluidity.* Arzneimittelforschung, 2001. **51**(2): p. 104-11.

32. Oh, J.Y., et al., *Antioxidant activity of olive flounder (Paralichthya olivaceus) surimi digest in in vitro and in vivo.* J Food Sci Technol, 2022. **59**(5): p. 2071-2079.

33. Diaz-Montana, E.J., et al., *Does A Flavoured Extra Virgin Olive Oil Have Higher Antioxidant Properties?* Antioxidants (Basel), 2022. **11**(3).

34. Davis, C., et al., *Definition of the Mediterranean Diet; a Literature Review.* Nutrients, 2015. **7**(11): p. 9139-53.

35. Acquistucci, R., et al., *Chemical, technological, and nutritional characteristics of two lines of "farro" (Triticum turgidum ssp. dicoccum).* Nahrung, 2004. **48**(3): p. 213-7.

36. Liu, T., et al., *Preparation, Characterization, and Antioxidant Activity of Nanoemulsions Incorporating Lemon Essential Oil.* Antioxidants (Basel), 2022. **11**(4).

37. Rashid, H.M., et al., *Antioxidant and Antiproliferation Activities of Lemon Verbena (Aloysia citrodora): An In Vitro and In Vivo Study.* Plants (Basel), 2022. **11**(6).

38. Pieroni, A., N. Sulaiman, and R. Soukand, *Chorta (Wild Greens) in Central Crete: The Bio-Cultural Heritage of a Hidden and Resilient Ingredient of the Mediterranean Diet.* Biology (Basel), 2022. **11**(5).

39. Stark, P.B., et al., *Open-source food: Nutrition, toxicology, and availability of wild edible greens in the East Bay.* PLoS One, 2019. **14**(1): p. e0202450.

40  Lo Bosco, F., et al., *Nutraceutical Value of Pantelleria Capers (Capparis spinosa L.).* J Food Sci, 2019. **84**(8): p. 2337-2346.

41  Ozcan, M.M., *Investigation on the mineral contents of capers (Capparis spp.) seed oils growing wild in Turkey.* J Med Food, 2008. **11**(3): p. 596-9.

42  Rachwa-Rosiak, D., E. Nebesny, and G. Budryn, *Chickpeas-composition, nutritional value, health benefits, application to bread and snacks: a review.* Crit Rev Food Sci Nutr, 2015. **55**(8): p. 1137-45.

43  Katsouri, E., et al., *Nutritional Characteristics of Prepacked Feta PDO Cheese Products in Greece: Assessment of Dietary Intakes and Nutritional Profiles.* Foods, 2020. **9**(3).

44  Silva, P. and N. Latruffe, *Benefits of the Mediterranean Diet-Wine Association: The Role of Ingredients.* Molecules, 2022. **27**(4).

45  Itsiopoulos, C., H.L. Mayr, and C.J. Thomas, *The anti-inflammatory effects of a Mediterranean diet: a review.* Curr Opin Clin Nutr Metab Care, 2022.

46  Cowell, O.R., et al., *Effects of a Mediterranean diet on blood pressure: a systematic review and meta-analysis of randomized controlled trials and observational studies.* J Hypertens, 2021. **39**(4): p. 729-739.

47  Papadaki, A., E. Nolen-Doerr, and C.S. Mantzoros, *The Effect of the Mediterranean Diet on Metabolic Health: A Systematic Review and Meta-Analysis of Controlled Trials in Adults.* Nutrients, 2020. **12**(11).

48  Coelho-Junior, H.J., A. Trichopoulou, and F. Panza, *Cross-sectional and longitudinal associations between adherence to Mediterranean diet with physical performance and cognitive function in older adults: A systematic review and meta-analysis.* Ageing Res Rev, 2021. **70**: p. 101395.

49  Mentella, M.C., et al., *Cancer and Mediterranean Diet: A Review.* Nutrients, 2019. **11**(9).

50 Barak, Y. and D. Fridman, *Impact of Mediterranean Diet on Cancer: Focused Literature Review.* Cancer Genomics Proteomics, 2017. **14**(6): p. 403-408.

51 Battino, M. and M.S. Ferreiro, *Ageing and the Mediterranean diet: a review of the role of dietary fats.* Public Health Nutr, 2004. **7**(7): p. 953-8.

52 Asbaghi, O., et al., *Effects of the Mediterranean diet on cardiovascular risk factors in non-alcoholic fatty liver disease patients: A systematic review and meta-analysis.* Clin Nutr ESPEN, 2020. **37**: p. 148-156.

53 Soltani, S., et al., *Adherence to the Mediterranean Diet in Relation to All-Cause Mortality: A Systematic Review and Dose-Response Meta-Analysis of Prospective Cohort Studies.* Adv Nutr, 2019. **10**(6): p. 1029-1039.

54 Garcia-Hermoso, A., et al., *Is adherence to the Mediterranean diet associated with healthy habits and physical fitness? A systematic review and meta-analysis including 565 421 youths.* Br J Nutr, 2020: p. 1-12.

55 Mancini, J.G., et al., *Systematic Review of the Mediterranean Diet for Long-Term Weight Loss.* Am J Med, 2016. **129**(4): p. 407-415 e4.

Soya Sauce — 2 tbsp  
Cornflour — 2 tbsp  
Ketchup — 60g  
Pineapple juice — 150ml  
Vinegar — 3 tbsp  
350ml Water

} ½ recipe for 2 people

2 pts/person.